Ground State

Ground State

Merrill Elizabeth Gray

Copyright © 2023 by Merrill Elizabeth Gray

All rights reserved. No part of this book may be reproduced or transmitted in any form or by any means without written permission from the author.

Scripture quotations are from the Holy Bible, New International Version®, NIV® Copyright ©1973, 1978, 1984, 2011 by Biblica, Inc.® Used by permission. All rights reserved worldwide.

Cover design: MiblArt

Editor: Lorna Stuber

ISBN (paperback): 978-1-7389622-0-4

For my children and grandchildren.

Table of Contents

I. Ground Level

Winter Ceremonies I	1
Redemption	3
Playing Doctor	4
Childcraft Encyclopedia	5
Holy Cow	6
Strange Ghosts	7
Speaking Part	8
Blinded by the Light	9
He Never Came Back	10

II. Ground Down

The Prize Cat	13
Pack Your Bags	15
They Said	17
Kalem	18
When I miss my kids	19
Baby Ballet	20
Hutterite girl 1 and Hutterite girl 2	21

III. Hunting Ground

Little Wing	25
Animal Instincts	26
Blank Canvas	27
Smug as a Bug	28
Housework	29
Saving Energy	30
Gone Astray	31
Yanking it	33
Mr. Clean	34
After the Fall	35
Elements	36
Twenty-Five Years	37
It's my divorce and I'll self-pity if I want to	38
How love works	40

IV. Proving Ground

    See you tomorrow Hayden Carruth   43
    Tightpantsrant   44
    Just Deserts   45
    Leaving earth before you planned   47
    Wondering   48
    How to get a poem published   49
    Bloom   51
    A dissimilar memory glosa   52
    Advice to a young girl   54

V. Ground Rules

    Enough War   59
    Scent   60
    A language unknown to me   61
    Ornithophobia   62
    Fortunate   63
    A Pantoum behaving badly   64
    The Ballad of Ruby Rush   65
    Oh Ruby   66
    Tape up the cupboards Liz we're moving   67
    Where are you going with your eight-piece place setting?   68
    Strays   69
    Whoa Nellie!   71

VI. High Ground

    Purge   77
    Mimic Poem   78
    Birds   80
    Aria Buffa   81
    Beast in the Bush   82
    Passover   83
    Tinder Love   84
    St. Peter's Abbey   85
    Get an opt out   86
    At the Guggenheim in Venice 2015   87
    To a Blind Woman   88
    Off on a Tangent   89
    Amendment   90

Mother's Prayer	91
Sweat	92
You are my Sunshine	94
Numbers and Hallways	95
That you died on a Sunday	96
The Abyssinian Baptist Church Harlem	97
Winter Ceremonies II	98

I. Ground Level

There's no truth about your childhood, though there's a story, yours to tend.

—William Matthews, *A Happy Childhood*

Winter Ceremonies I

Forty below with wind chill
frozen feet in plastic boots
scarf caught in tow rope
dragged up the hill

This strangling life
I see your
Sasquatch figure
ominous
at the bottom of
White Track
Get back up there you say
I paid for this

Orange shag
brown sofa
my brother and I
circle the house
chasing each other
until I crash through
the ornate gold divider

Stop
footsteps thunder on the stairs
welts on our skin
imprints of a gaudy era

When I was seven, my father tried to drown me
he walked into the lake
dunked me under
repeatedly

he wanted to see me struggle, turn blue
bloated
float away
his problems gone

I don't know what stopped him
he could have easily done me in

there were times I wished he would have ended it

Redemption

Hard pews
hot black gowns
hymn books
high pitched voices
irrelevant babble

All those stifling Sundays

None as significant
as the shriek of the cat
caught in the fan belt
blood-spattered
leg-severed

Rescued
in your respectable
rabbit skin fur coat

Saved by amputation

Playing Doctor

we played in the turret house
where drapes flapped at windows
like the false eyelashes of ghosts

we crept up the winding stairs

hush hush

your yellow cotton candy hair
stick legs in a plaid skort
my bruises
bathed in rags
needed repair

I laid on the examining table
a broken corpse

you planted the Smartie like a seed
in the soft creases
of my mouth which had not yet spoken

I held it tight inside me until it melted
wanting so badly to be healed

Childcraft Encyclopedia

How was I to love reading
      when words were swathed in
      red and white hard-covered facts
A prestige purchase from a traveling salesman
      Filed neatly in their wooden rack
      inclined like an easy-boy chair
      beside the black and white tv
After reading them from cover to cover
      I craved more
      to inhale the glossy pages
to stroke them blithely like I was reading Braille

I strayed down dog-filled streets
      to the Public Library
      at Crescent Park
      pushing a stroller
      permission to go granted
if I took my baby brother to see the swans

It was back when
you could buy ten candy cigarettes for a nickel
      there were no child abusers running rampant
      children did what they were told
      read only what they could gather off the shelves
and juggle all the way home

Holy Cow

In winter
you did donuts on the frozen pond with the skidoo
hear that you said
waiting for the ice to crack
before revving up the hill

then in summer
on your mini-scooter in the wheat fields
grasshoppers leapt at my legs
left red marks like chickenpox

I had asked to see the boys at the next farm
it was worth it

In your green army jeep
we rose and fell
on the scorching metal seats
at each crest of the dirt road
dust harvested a storm wherever we went

we picked rocks
made our own Stonehenge and later
consumed crabapples until our stomachs ached

you showed me your prize kill
hides hung in the shed by the barn
sold for cash
you should buy a cow you said

I'm a kid from the city
this holy farm life
an unfamiliar sacrament

Strange Ghosts

Hanging in mid-air, you swung me, my ribs crushed on the bottom of your feet. I didn't care that it hurt; I was flying. Round and round we laughed until the wind blew right out of us. And then on the backyard pavement we were film directors. I gave myself the lead role. Appeared like magic from under the table through the make shift curtain; an old blanket with holes big enough to see a clown's eye through. Except there wasn't a clown and we were pretending to be happy.

Speaking Part

I was the director
of the backyard circus

spewed orders
to neighborhood kids

an action figure on a bike
at the playground
picked up sticks spinning
on the merry-go-round
until I puked

at the rink shack shouted
hail hail the gang's all here
what the hell do we care

even when you told me not to

I made up my life

Blinded by the Light

on Christmas morning
wound up we woke at 3AM to
peek at Santa's thoughtfulness

only to be told we had to
get back upstairs and wait
for the camera to capture our innocence

march down the stairs in perfect formation
oldest first
act like we are the luckiest children on this planet

blinded by this ceremony of happiness
as the flash pulsated

this might be the only time we get
to reenact joy

He Never Came Back

he drove away
like Jed Clampett in his hillbilly mobile
and I pretended not to know him
not that he made promises
no attempts at love

he questioned that
from his gene pool befell
a book daughter
a walk in from a world of words
always questioning
his position

it's no wonder
he couldn't stand the pressure
said *I never should have been a parent*
steered away from responsibility
hit the road

II. Ground Down

You remember through a filter of self. The periods in your life when that self is half formed, your memories are half formed too.

—Mary Karr

The Prize Cat

a mash up poem inspired by E.J. Pratt

1973
Analyze the poem, she said

I was an optimistic poet studying Canadian Poetry

I searched for answers in the stacks of the library periodical room
        no google god would save me

I observed "*The Prize Cat demonstrates an instant reversal to primal nature in a pet that has been tamed and comes from a pure blood line.*"[1]

Held my hand high, "*The human race is primal and uses instinctive needs as well as ethics in order to survive and progress.*"[2]

"No it's not about that!" a *sudden sharp assault.*

"Could it not also be about human relationships?" I said *gentility was in the fur.*

"Is that the best you can do?" *she gleamed.*

"*Though it pertains to a prize-tabby yet it also applies to the most cultivated of the human species, male and female.*"[3]

"No, you are wrong!" *the jungle strains within the cells* and in veins of her throat.

"Certainly there are different levels of meaning in the poem?" I said *soft-mannered, musical in purr.*

"*You are wrong! It refers to Mussolini's attack on Ethiopia just before the Second World War.*"

Her eyes rolled back in a trance and *caught me on the wing.*

"You. Get out!" *anger ever arched her back.* "Get out of my class!"

"*The sudden assault implies colossal powers uncontrolled and irresistible—not just out there in*

the external world but here, close by, inside the domestic cat and within our own civilized self."[4]

From behind the desk came the leap *so furtive-wild.*

"Why don't you just go home and have babies!" she hissed.

And crying *like an Abyssinian child had cried out in the whitethroat's scream.*

That's exactly what I did.

Pack Your Bags

No matter what you do

take it upon yourself to travel

catch a train and jump off whenever

it stops

quickly
        you might not have much

time to enter every cathedral

        when the organist is practicing

and the afternoon sunlight is

        shining through God's arms

kneel down like you mean it

even if you've never sung a hymn

sing
        to yourself, and count your blessings

eat ratatouille

say French words like voila and moi bien

smoke Gitane cigarettes

drink lemonade while you lounge

        topless on the beach in Biarritz

ride a scooter but don't get too close

        to the edge

hold your passport near your heart

and come back to me

They Said

The Doctor in his white arrogance
said
I don't understand why you're so upset

The Nurse in her heavenly benevolence
said
It was God's will

The Mother in her vast experience
said
It happened, get over it

My heart's loss so immense
said
My child is gone

You
held my sobbing hand
said
We'll have another

Kalem

I used to keep you

in the cradle right beside my bed

arm's length

breath in sync with mine

now you are a day ahead of me

far away

arms extended

When I miss my kids

at night

you warm my side of the bed to take away my chills

in the morning

you sing to me of *golden daffodils*

and memories of green rolling hills

while I curl into a fetal position

gasp for air

Baby Ballet

perfectly turned-out legs
pointed genetic toes

pirouette on the change table
plié at the crib bar

you wobble on the world

equilibrium
more poised than mine

you know mommy
laugh at my hang-ups
my twirled reality

already

you know the dance of life

Hutterite girl 1 and Hutterite girl 2

You tell me your favorite songs
your cell phone numbers
dreams of travel

escape

not so different than other girls

You tell me your homework will be late
It's been busy on the farm

You tell me that I am your line of communication
to the outside world and that the
Colony Minister ruled that you cannot
stay in school beyond grade ten
studying English Literature is not important
German would be better

I don't want you to stay   there

I don't want to let you go

III. Hunting Ground

The infinite capacity of humans to wound one another without meaning or wanting to.

—Margaret Laurence, *The Diviners*

Little Wing

Point Pelee is home to three hundred and seventy species of birds

      I will learn their names

pause my life   hover like a shiny black cormorant (double-crested)

a surveyor of new terrain—

You marched on ahead of me

      studying the facts

           —focused on your personal geography

astounded to be standing at the same latitude as San Francisco

I hobbled behind — burning my feet on the sand

      holding our child

my flip-flop broken after flailing into Lake Erie to rescue him

he waded beyond the hazard sign and almost tumbled off

      the edge of the earth

That is what it felt like. Standing on the rim looking out—

      I could have lost him

      I had already lost you

Animal Instincts

One in the morning
        the space beside me is vacant

unsettling light
        peers through the crack under the bedroom door

I catch you
        watching reruns of a nova science series
                some Darwin special on survival of the species

I'm not sure what the attraction is
        the aggressive hunt for their next kill
                or the screams of elk humping in mating season

Go back to sleep I'll be up soon you say

my fleshy body flails
        unshaven legs rub against the sunburnt sheets
                I cup my pubic bone with one hand
                      hold my heart with the other

a beast in the basement howls
        thumps up the stairs
                comes to our bed

under your T-shirt
        I seek solace
                in your blue ox shape
                discover
            more hair on your back
                than there used to be

Blank Canvas

I wanted to render the landscape
as easily as rotating a kaleidoscope.
Amass arbitrary patterns: sprinkle in
the changing seasons with a brush stroke. Blue

intersected by ginger leaves. Stipples of unruffled winds exhaling
smidges of pine scents. Below broad strokes of barren beaches where
young lovers lolled, wrapped in Cowichan knit sweaters serenaded
by James Taylor singing *you've got a friend.*

I should not have used black paint: got carried away
with small arrow shapes that started out as birds, shrouded
the entire sky and swathed the field
like a flock of geese. Until

it was one immense black hole

        I fell
into
        You

seized my arm on the downward spiral,

don't cut off your ear yet

Smug as a Bug

My husband says that living with a poet
is just one big thrill

that he never knows what will
spurt from my volcano self

what hot lava will
engulf him
what words of wisdom will
wallop him

his mind's eye pierced like a prism punched by the sun

he's not warming up to the idea

he watches what he thinks now

Housework

I can't do anything anymore without stopping
to write a poem
words creep into my mind on waking
hardly time to shower
I write and write and write
until my wrists hurt

time waits for me
but I tell it to go ahead

I must sit and brood in this uncomfortable chair called memory
until the pain in me is splattered on the page
black and white
almost
makes me want to vacuum

Saving Energy

You tell me that you want to live off grid

go Amish—stop wearing anything with zippers

I think   how convenient

You buy every book possible on saving energy

I think   waste of paper

You want to plant hemp maybe some marijuana

I think   good idea

Then you change your mind

still need cash to put the kids through college

Now you peddle yellow destructive machines that

Build capitalistic dreams

Now I flounder my socialist ways   here and there

    Spend $350 on a pair of Frye boots

I fantasize wearing them on that acreage

To wander in my own field of dreams

    To search for secrets in your trousers

    And sample the abundance

Gone Astray

I lost you when the season turned itself over

when the trees waved goodbye

    to green and their

proud black branches bent over

    copper discards cried for cover and waited

for secure white blankets to warm them

you said there was a heart in the tree you photographed

you said hope is not a plan

but for now

    it's the only plan I have

I plan to find someone to hibernate with

to roll their secure body next

    to mine

    so that

my blooms are not bound like leaking breasts

the seeping nectar will warm our winter souls

    and later plant seeds in our garden

I plan to move on because I know

that I cannot stay in this leafy uncertainty

at least the season holds a promise of returning, but not you

Yanking it

Served up between the stacks like two olives and a cock
tail sausage
you want them to notice your obsession
with yourself

it's just a slab of skin
lying dead like a fish washed up on shore
gills heaving

and then
your thrills were stopped
you flashed the wrong girl
You were tracked down
security called
your exhibitionist life
over

Mr. Clean

you used to rub me in all the right places
now your touch
is as abrasive as comet cleanser
you ran your finger over my body looking for dust
imperfect as a cracked cup
you were my white knight
now you are darkness
a shade of my existence
I erase

you used to write me love letters
now your word
is as vile as spit
you censured my voice
suppressed me like a banned book
you were my confidante
now you are foe
a stain on my presence
I remove

you used to give me compliments
now your voice
is as impersonal as steel
you regurgitated my secrets
like unpleasant medicine
you were my warm thoughts
now you are rime
a splotch on my past
I eliminate
no more Mr. Clean

After the Fall

I hand you the words that were locked in my mind's prison
words that knocked at the cell door, they were

constantly rapping, tapping away
like I have all the time in the world to

listen to them preach their pain
to look at them and contemplate the

order I should put them in, yet each
wants to be first and

I can't decide
like in a frustrating dream when

nothing goes the way it should and I try
to make them sound good together, smooth

like a newly washed floor I want
them to gleam, shed some light on

your mind when I hand you my poems
longing for you to love me

Elements

Even if I look as far as I can across
the lake I cannot see the

future, the vacant hills tell me
that you will not be

in it, so my life is given to the
wind and the sun

appears only when I
deserve it

you might not think
that I can see you, but through the green

forest, the water moves
toward me, I would like to be completely

covered by the waves, then I
would float away

to a place where you would not exist
my heart never again cut

into small bits
and laid on the sand to dry

Twenty-Five Years

If I could sing to you
my voice would be Eva Cassidy's
I would capture your heart with my songs
like water gathers sand
and pull you under
you would be my Hummingbird
and I your sugar pot

We would wander through the grasses
let nature find a clearing
we would fall back in longing
like curls of loose hair
and touch each other's paradise
you would be my Bumblebee
and I your Morning Glory

If I could be your songbird
I'd sing you a smooth one
I'd belt out jazz licks
like Ella Fitzgerald
and embrace your fragile soul
you would be my Robin
and I your fresh worm

We would choose our own pathway
let the stars guide us
we would soar through life
like Eagles
you would be my harmony
and I your sweet, sweet melody

It's my divorce and I'll self-pity if I want to

Your spouse will tell you about their many affairs
You will get a lawyer and pay with money you have to borrow
You will kick your spouse out of the family home
You will be told by your lawyer that everything is split equally
You will not get support because you have worked for thirty years
Your accountant will tell you to *run*
You will get your name off his business debt
You will get to keep some of your own pension
You will be discarded by your former family
You will hear lies

After the divorce
You will be blamed
You will not be asked how you are
You will be shamed out of town
You will be cancelled
You will get PTSD
You will change your name and move to another province
You will think you have time to find a new relationship (you never will)
You will work two jobs to support yourself and try to retire before you turn seventy

After the divorce
You will be 'I'
You will grieve
You will go for counselling
You will be hollow
You will be isolated
You will not get invited to couples' events
You will not trust
You will not date
You will be told to get over it
You will not want to talk about it anymore

Your former friends will support your ex and attend his wedding to the person whom he cheated with for years

They will justify this by saying *well he never really did anything to me*

In front of your children, they will say *their dad finally found the love of his life*

You will be asked why you are still single

You will laugh!

How love works

Snow be gone
stop fluttering around my murky mind

these winter days and nights blur together
dark and listless like soggy mulch

the seasons change to remind us
that love will come again

bloom like perennials beckoning
green from the soil of our frozen hearts

tell me you love me because
spring is coming

IV. Proving Ground

In your life there are a few places, or maybe only the one place, where something happened, and then there are all the other places.

—Alice Munro, *Too Much Happiness*

See you tomorrow Hayden Carruth

> *The next time you see a line*
> *Of geezers shuffling toward the check-out*
> *Remember they are entering the arcade of*
> *Death*
> —Hayden Carruth

The next time you see me
I'll be the one with crippled fingers
spent too much time at the computer
punching out my reality
I'll be hobbling beside you
holding your words
And wondering what they mean
Day after day

My friends say my writing is too dark
and I think of what you said
That you can't blame the poet
more than the rest

and I feel comforted that I will not
cause the fallout
will not be responsible
for their delusions

and I hope to see you tomorrow
in that floating cloud of poets
looking down on earth and
thumping people on the head saying
wake up
wake up
what the hell are you thinking

Tightpantsrant

It usually happens on a day when you have a spring in your step and you feel a like the sun is shining just for you and you've decided to take up yoga and you wander into a store to buy the latest tight pants and the girl says to you oh yes, those are the style that my mom wears. You're sure she is just trying to be pleasant, to strike up a conversation maybe make a sale. But it hits you like a stone pinging off your windshield and yes indeed she has put you in the same age category as her mother. She is not one of the younger attendants in the store; she appears to be the store manager and she's likely younger than your oldest daughter. Wait for it—she can't stop herself: I hope I look as good as you when I'm your age. (You want to say you don't look as good as me now). You are a middle-aged woman and every style in the store makes it even more prominent. That pulpy protuberance that reminds you that you gave birth to three children, endured twenty-five years of not sleeping through the night and have been too tired for exercise of any kind. Even though you want the glow of downward dog, and the yoga instructor is the cutest young guy you have seen half naked in forty years, you just don't know if your back can handle all that twisting and turning. And you ponder skipping yoga and going to a friend's for a glass of wine instead. You need it more than falling on your head while attempting a handstand against a wall. Somehow you have made it. Burned your bra, survived all of the fads, and still you spend over one hundred dollars on tight pants and they come with a bag that chants your outlook on life is a reflection of how much you like yourself and breathe deeply and do one thing a day that scares you like reading the words will make you a better person. You have just purchased happiness and a chance to get rid of the ripples of cellulite that hang in layered folds under your arms and besides, your ass looked pretty damn good in the three-way mirror and low lights. Tight pants that clinch caesarean closures and bind the breach of a bewildered bulky uterus that was wrenched out like a woolly sweater (it was just hanging around too full of itself). And you wonder if she will ever thank you.

Just Deserts

My mother always forgets that I dislike Christmas pudding

every year she says *I didn't know that* and then serves it to me anyway

a fine china bowl of overcooked mushy cake with unrecognizable emerald bits

and a syrupy sauce

she spent months preparing—

I take a few small bites

It's the least I can do

Now I find I do the same thing with my adult children

forget their likes and dislikes —tomatoes, olives, red meat

forget which one fractured their wrist, leg, collarbone

whose pain I suffered more

I am humiliated by memory, grasp

apologize

It's all I can do

They remind me that

she was not a perfect parent

I am not a perfect parent

That our children have their own lives to digest

Leaving earth before you planned

Life kissed you

your last child barely off your breast

tiny fingers still grasped

there was nothing

you did or didn't do

death beat your bones like back labor

you flailed here and there

wanted to turn out the light

and suddenly like paper whisking in a breeze

no one could catch

you fluttered away

Wondering

> *Well, my mother was a prisoner.*
> *She was a captive of her upwardly mobile yearnings.*
> —Maxine Kumin

At the point in life
when you have nothing

to lose, I wonder when you say
you are just *writing what is wrung from you*

if you are an old dish rag worn because
you washed the way for us, leaving

holes deep in your soul, so that women can
stop living in a laundry commercial and

start enjoying life
and I wonder when the pills we took to buy

this freedom, will stop causing concaves the size of
moon craters in our bodies

How to get a poem published

I

Write a long poem in stanzas announced with roman numerals
long enough for people to feel the agony, the ecstasy, and the journey
long enough for them to understand the meaning or at least think about
it
use words like cacophony and obliquely
add some alliteration—a few metaphors or similes
   —words   like   steps   on a ladder
be like those poets who say they don't know where the poem comes
from—it just
coalesces like fine dew drops forming delicious patterns
they might say something like *that was distinctive and inimitable*

II

Write a poem that shows how life unraveled right before your eyes; make
sure
that you *show not tell* so they believe you
and do not question your truth or say *that never really happened you must be
lying*
make their minds wander off to question
   —their own aggregate entity
because you know they are self-absorbed and really, they want to know
it's all about them
they might ask silly questions like *what is the essence of the poem?*

III

Write a poem with big words, allude to some other time in history,
perhaps add a few scholarly names like Solomon Schechter, scientific
names, minerals like sanidine or corundum, places they have never
heard of like Bomarzo, names they won't even recognize and they have
to look up
they might say *wow that was clever* or perhaps they will not say it was clever
but at least say *that was peculiarly deep.*

IV

Write a poem that rescues you from the emotional bursts you are used to writing
maybe even place one word standing
Alone.
They like that. One person looking out over the sea—dipping their toe in the vast blue.
Sometimes use rhyming words; magical, radical, comical words or misplaced and awkward
words, not-even-making-sense words, Patois that pitter-patter like petite rap music
they might say *Oh my.*

V

Write a poem like Ferlinghetti —or maybe try another nutty beat poet or maybe cummings but
do not attempt Stevens
put in some commas, and dashes —or use a hyphen-
just to throw them off
maybe even add a semicolon; now that would be a shock
they might say *wow this writer knows how to get a poem published (or perhaps Microsoft Word does)*

VI

Write a poem in a form that is recognized and accepted
note what is published in the literary journals
the snobby pretentious ones
the really full-of-themselves ones that sit on the edge of the ocean like whales and spout
partial knowledge because what they say counts and eventually, after they read your bio, after
many attempts to please them, they might say *you are good enough to be published*

Bloom

The naturopath said you don't like wearing turtlenecks
        because you had a bad birth experience

    Did I?

Yes, you had the cord around your neck
        I had to stop pushing or I might have killed you
The obstetrician untangled you from an estranged place
        heaved you out screaming

    I'm here but I'm there as well

You grew like a dandelion determined not to be a weed
        Yellow sparks   little blossoms

I should have named you Daisy

Later, you wrote in a language I did not understand
        b d and p identical triplets to you—
        Mine was not your mother tongue

You spoke spirit—
    Grandma is going to die

    One day later she did

Then, she muttered to you from the afterlife—
        I overheard snippets of long conversations—
    Ears extended

    Grey voices   little whispers

I pined to be part of your words

What did grandma say? I asked

    It's okay to pick the flowers

A dissimilar memory glosa

> *The silence of earth is now your silence,*
> *After which there is neither dirge nor cheer.*
> *There are other games, other silences,*
> *But none so still as that which lingers here.*
>   —Glen Sorestad, *Elegy for Sondra*

She's dead they said
and I did not believe them
still
   do not believe them
my thoughts were
concealed in my conscience
I should have spoken out against tradition
stopped the clash of her desires and their hate
given her guidance
The silence of earth is now your silence

I should have made sure she could get in
should have checked
should have been there when she huddled
   alone in the garage
trying to stay warm
it was not clear
and there was no tomorrow
no laughter no celebration
no grade twelve year
After which there is neither dirge nor cheer

I cannot think of
her without welling up
tears like salty sea water
        sting
obstruct my throat
yet, her voice influences
me, tells me to
carry on   carry on
find other accomplices
there are other games, other silences

In my Elegy for Sondra
I endure a dissimilar memory
I suffer her promise
        my heart a silent murmur
picked up the beat where hers ceased
and all these years
she exhaled through my skin
her spirit strolled in my bones
I still hear her tears
But none so still as that which lingers here

Advice to a young girl

Communicate now only through translations
vanished like virgin fears
unraveled
all coincidences dissolved
by your presence
....

particles of ice dissolved on the pane
slabs of snow slid from branches

exhausted   draped nude

night cried where he dug a hole

she noticed the earrings on the bedside table

not hers

morning caught her in her own bed
....

a drug-induced state
to dull your creative mind
put on those real fake nails
strum that guitar
dig deep
find that inner voice
you are Roberta Flack
killing me softly
over
and
over again
....

Freedom
if you're a bird
and only need a wire for comfort
and a flock to survive
is fine
freedom is fine
....

bad weekend
preoccupied with uncouth language
perverse staleness
tell you where his ego leaks
you might want to avoid more slime
....

You finally have it
it's not they who do not understand you
it's you who does not understand what they guess is you and it's you
who guesses that they think you're the way they see you
it's them thinking that they understand what you know isn't you
and it's you confused between what's really you and what they see you as
....

Saturday morning coffee interrupted by
Jehovah's Witness at her door

Telling her Jesus is coming to her community
She tells them she is a

girl with no voice
tiptoeing like a squirrel grabbing small bits

to fill her emptiness

she is saying the right prayer
to the right God

Go ahead
you may tell her your story
but don't tell her what she won't want to hear

V. Ground Rules

Grief, when it comes, is nothing like we expect it to be.

—Joan Didion

Enough War

we slept on a futon on the floor
your sheepdog snoring nearby
not a care in the world

we slept on a hand-me-down mattress
our children breathing nearby
not a care in the world

we have a king-size bed now
you do aerobics every night
and I can never sleep

the space between us a demilitarized zone
I wait for you to send out Morse code
and sometimes I parachute over

Scent

You left your pillow
at the hotel

Carried it with you on road trips
Needed to be comforted by yourself

Every morning in my marriage ritual
I rolled over and breathed in your smells

Your pillow had them all stored up
Twenty-seven years of collecting you

and now it lies
at the hotel desk lost and found

You didn't go back or couldn't

You left your smell with strangers and
returned home to me

A language unknown to me

You kill a centipede in the basement. I call it a Seahorse.

I don't know why? It just came galloping out of my mouth.

You can hardly control yourself, laughing, holding onto your
       broken rib so that it doesn't burst through your blasé skin.

Oh it's not the first time I've blurted out an improper word.

There was that cantaloupe running in the wheat field;
       the man with an Aztec around his neck.

I'm lost in a lexicon, speaking in tongues,
       a language you try to interpret.

You like to think you have one up on me. You do mathematical calculations.
       Sudoku. Backgammon. Cribbage.

All that adding: I try to ignore fifteen two fifteen four.

I play at random; you hate it when I win.

       You can't even add you say.

You keep tabs on me now

       worry that I might actually have early Alzheimer's, although

       it's not so early anymore.

Ornithophobia

Seagulls monopolize the beach like baby boomers in Florida

hundreds of them
      a mob
scouring for leftovers
chips and apple cores
      fooled by candy wrappers

they point toward us and strut in slow steps
webbed feet and tiny talons sidestep on the sand

auricular puffed up   bellies concaved
      form straight lines like an army

A few have seen better days
      faded plumage
        scruffy grey scapulars
necks palsy with delirium tremors
like they had been out all night on a bender

Some swoop down and pull weeds from the lake
      taunt others
      pretend they scored

They respect our space but
wait patiently to peck at our flesh
Their beady little eyes
bills pursed ready to aim   mandibles open
they hold their tight cloaca vent
ready to let the bomb drop or transfer sperm like firing a missile

They rise as a group in flight
      each followed after each
        a line against the sunset
          nature's perfect geometry

Fortunate

1.
wet cement and sand fell off the house like cold porridge.
you stole the supplies and left a bag of nails then wanted more money sent an
email message THIS IS JESUS I LOST YOUR NUMBER CALL ME.

2.
proud of your polished expressions; how many days did you lumber in the maze of words
lost in a lexicon *not all poets are lunatics*
just some   just some

A Pantoum behaving badly

he shampooed his way into her life
his monstrous arm swung like a crane
caused a colossal amount of strife
the falling out left a stain

his monstrous arm swung like a crane
she only had herself to blame
the falling out left a stain
she even tried to file a claim

she only had herself to blame
her luck would soon run dry
she even tried to file a claim
they would believe his lie

her luck would soon run dry
no proof of his abuse
they would believe his lie
she would have to cut him loose

no proof of his abuse
when he shampooed his way into her life
that she would have to cut him loose
caused a colossal amount of strife

The Ballad of Ruby Rush

Good land at low prices they said
new opportunity,
great ruby red rock full of quartz
promised prosperity.

Ruby Rush held out her hand with
the allure of pleasure.
She promised more than good fortune
with garnets of treasure.

The prospectors flowed into town
Gordon boys laid their claim,
and when most left empty-handed
Harris was left the blame.

Embarrassed by the incident
not talked about for years,
descendants still lived near the town
old wounds still full of fears.

And so seventy years later
they talk of history,
and the museum in Harris tells
the Ruby Rush story.

The annual Ruby Rush Days
once were a whispered hush,
now celebrate with vignette plays
about the Ruby Rush.

Oh Ruby

you held treasures in your soil

your garnets glowed like red hair drunk on rain

you proposed promises of gold

and waved your wealthy hand like wheat

blowing on the prairie beckoning

over here   over here

men came

when they were wasted on wine

they paid to view your splendor

when your canny hoax held pebbles of despair

they scorned your sultry charm

you whispered

hush hush

don't tell the tale of the Ruby Rush

Tape up the cupboards Liz we're moving

And off they went in a
65 Chevrolet station wagon
with the bowler trailer flippin' around
behind them

Leaving another prairie tumbleweed town
that blew gossip like churchwomen
at the Sunday bizarre

He'd traded in the 57' Oldsmobile for it
the one they played in while he sat in the bar drinking
from 11AM-11PM every day
until he was either
thrown out
passed out
carried out

they still let him drive
with his five kids in the back seat
crammed so close they clung to each other
for fear the doors might fall open
and out they would tumble

Liz kept the duct tape handy
sometimes not even removing it from the cupboards

Where are you going with your eight-piece place setting?

Eight pearly semi-porcelain plates
large-rimmed abundance
your chipped life swirled
and dug in like sand-etching

why bother carefully packing them
just throw them in the back seat of the car

the gourmet cook has left the building
spices and oils dripping over gold embossing
reminds you of
his tasteless lying life

you leave him the Corning Ware® and
a can of olives

Strays

If our ancestors knew their fate was eternal

would they have embarked on their journey over water
        left unstable continents for the promised land

would they have taken the chance
        that their children and children after
        would never cut loose
        from patterns they stitched in their stockings
        carried with them like smallpox

their homestead produced nothing
        more than weeds
        their foundation proved not
        as strong as dirt

it should have held them tight, but
        thrust them across the prairies
        by boxcar
        off and on they jumped

settlers who never settled

        drank too much

        smoked too much

They could not exhale properly

        no air exchange in their oral history

        no breathing room

It was in the leaving that they discovered why

        They could not suppress their past

Divorce deep-rooted in every generation
    Or Suicide

Neither a good choice

Whoa Nellie!

In memory of Nellie Lavinia Ferneyhough Pell
1897-1991

She crossed the Atlantic on the Cunard Line in 1928, 3rd class
On a two-foot-wide berth for twelve days
No water, soap or towels
Food sparse
In Montreal, she cut her glossy black waist-length hair into a stylish bob
Traveled by train to Moose Jaw
A prairie lily on unstable soil
She met farmer
Arthur Pell at a dance hall

Busily she birthed three daughters
On their homestead of silt floors
Later, moved to Brownlee into a house with an oval glass door
Bluebird salt and pepper shakers kissed on the window sill

When Arthur died young
She companion planted perennials in the dappled shade
Of her half-acre English Country garden

She
Never drove a vehicle
Never wore pants
Never voted
She stored produce in wooden crates in a moldy basement
Hauled water from the town well
Used the outhouse even after indoor plumbing was installed
Preferred a wood burning stove for heat
Slept on a cot in the spine of the hardhearted house

She didn't trust
Microwaves
Polyester
Food in tin cans
Cheese Whiz
Hotdogs and
One son in-law

She did not fear him though
She could kill a rat with a shovel
Her dog Twiggy took care of the snakes, tossing them in the air

5'1" with toiled hands, olive skin, dusty eyes
Her black hair now white as paper

We grandchildren shared cups of tea in Royal Albert Tea Rose china,
Nibbled on banana muffins while
Sitting pinched on a burgundy horse-hair sofa

She pruned us
Rooting our dreams with fables
Of Highbury Farm, Monmouth, Wales
Of being the youngest child in a family of ten
An after thought

If she could see us now
Still sprouting from her sown seeds
We are drought resistant,
We are light feeders and water wise
From one teensy woman sprouted sixty-one souls
Our feet firmly on her cultivated ground
Clump forming on the prairies

When she was ashes, she transmitted a message
through my young daughter,
'It's okay to pick the flowers.' And I did. I do.
Still, in my dreams she plucks my hand
and strives to take me some place
Not yet, Grandma, not yet

Well-hidden until her death at 94 years old,
Her birth certificate told the truth

She had dead-headed her illegitimate status in Wales

Some place
My great grandfathers
Blood line is scattered across Europe
Some where
His great and great great grandchildren
Budding in a faraway garden

VI. High Ground

Happiness is the lucky pane of glass you carry in your head. It takes all your cunning just to hang on to it, and once it's smashed you have to move into a different sort of life.

—Carol Shields, *Unless*

Purge

Instructions: Take digital photos and discard

Dolls in plastic cases never opened 1960
Drawing of a horse grade one 1963
A book report about Birds 1965
Life Magazine 'Off to the Moon' July 4, 1969 50 cents
Life Magazine 'Leaving the Moon' July 25, 1969 50 cents
A New Testament Bible 1970
Two black velvet paintings of children with large eyes 1970
A red silk smock dress with an embroidered rose 1972
A curling bag with Saskatchewan on one side
and maiden name on the other 1975
Two polyester jumpsuits circa 1976
Scrapbooks of a trip to Europe 1978
A French-English translation dictionary with print too small to read
even with 2.0 glasses
Diaries with no keys (no date)
Three bridesmaid dresses
    (yellow Swiss dot, orange and white swirled cape and turquoise
    green polyester)1980s
Essays written during multiple degrees at university 1978-2002
Jewelry made by hand in 1982
Cassette tapes 1990s
iPods that can't be charged 2001
Photo Albums 1985-2014

Now
buy five memory boxes for your three children,
yourself and your ex
Separate all the photos of him
    strategically
write on the back of each photo
this is when you were having an affair with 'G'
this is when you were having an affair with 'A'

Mimic Poem

"The Only Sign of Trauma" by Michelle Lesniak

I remember when the accountant said
You didn't hear this from me but run
How I ignored so many signs over the years; warnings about transgressions
And the lawyer said he really doesn't have to pay you anything
because you've worked for thirty years
I don't know what happened to the promises you made or why
You stopped making any promises at all
They seemed entirely believable, but I see how lying came easily to you
I remember noticing the slight changes
The pulling away and cutting comments
The only sign of trauma on an otherwise perfect love
This didn't bother you nearly as much as it bothered me
I remember shaking for most of the fallout
Because you have been scared since you were a child,
Because the inevitable was closing in around us,
Because nothing ever seemed real to you except your other life,
Its comfort, its familiarity, hard landing.
You tried to hide it from our home, but comments from family who
spotted your truck late at night in unknown places
jolted you awake like debt collectors
a reminder of the days you spent 'growing to hate me'
There was nothing that could convince you to kiss me
Not even the image of our children and their children, nothing about retirement or future plans
I remember you saying what's the point of doing an evaluation of the business that's two hundred thousand in debt
Coming home, everything was touched by your admitting, the way you planned to leave
And it was me struggling to split the empty assets,
And it was our fate,
And it was a thousand years of people not telling the truth,
And it was hidden, it was pride, it was tragic
The next time I dreamt of you it was you with him
I asked you why you kept your deep dark secret-fear or selfishness,

Or wanting both, or a thousand years of people not telling the truth,
I remember now that you had done this many times
I forget if I asked you before.

Birds

for Patrick Lane

When I think of you
        I think of illusory wilderness

of ships balancing on a tightrope horizon

of empty bottles wrapped in seaweed

of finding fragile gifts in foreign places

of blue butterflies

of seagulls swooping—dive bomb dispositions
       —almost attacking   then spiraling up to pink clouds

casting their feathers, their quills stick in the sand like a child's fort
       —almost buried by the waves   but still standing

You tell me not to lose the names of things
our vocabulary is in danger of being extinct
our images no longer described with words
our sentences confused by meaningless dashes—and semi-colons

we are northerners—visitors in our own land
living in imagined places—unreal
our rural world appears only on tv images
from the country south

You tell me that words will come—roll in like the tide

if I wait

wait to receive the story

wait for it

Aria Buffa

A man wearing a street dweller costume parades Granville
        performing a traveling opera recital
Animated like
        Charles Hardouin (French operatic baritone)

I walk by
        Ears gawking

He is the bellwether heralding change
        I want to join his gig like a sheep in his herd

What is his story line?
He could be a *walk in* from the 18th century
Recreating a scena
        A flowing cantabile

I'm a 21st century bystander
Stuck in the present day
My performance is stilted by hang ups
Self-doubt   uncertainty
        A timid trobairitz

This harbinger gestures toward me like a conductor
        arms deftly lifted
        whispers his message

It's a Ritornelli, you come in on the da capo, sing in a relative major key.

Beast in the Bush

    She walks everyday on a path that used to be a road near the lake. She stopped listening to her iPod since she spotted the timber wolf romping across the path the other day. A rare sighting. Usually there are elk or deer but she had never seen a wolf. At first, she thought it was a large German shepherd, off leash. Light cream legs delicate almost. Body, dappled brown and taupe, a black tip on the tail like it had been dipped in paint.

    Fir trees and birch blend together and shelter the creek. Interspersed dead trees look like black and white pencil drawings. Their trunks exposed now to the sky. Wind whirls the leaves that sound like rain, the flies swirl her head into a meditative state.

    The footsteps enter her ears and then her brain. She springs to the side of the path. Someone pushes her from behind and catches her off balance. Then grabs her arm and twists and thrusts her to the ground. Weeds with small white flowers meet her on the way down. He has on a white sleeveless gauzy shirt and tight spandex shorts. A sharp crack in the trees spooks him. He runs off. A deer crooks its head toward her. She stands up and meets the deer's perfectly round eyes. *Be careful; there are many beasts in the woods* said the deer. *Thanks for your help* she said back.

    Lately she has been into road kill. Watching for sightings, naming the animals, their half raspberry-colored bodies left for the ravens.

Passover

But woe to that man who betrays the Son of Man! It would be better for him if he had not been born. (Matthew 26:24)

My mom and I have two things in common

We look alike
        ginger hair and freckles
        now portly brown spots on our aging hands

And we both married con artists

We didn't know it at the time of course…fell for them like dogs for treats
we begged for more
believed them
became their
pillars
stood tall like disciples

We listened to them preach their sermons
trusted them

We dispensed their deceptions like bible salesman
        people abided

They were not good treasurers and we didn't audit them

They were patronizing thieves who pilfered our money, embezzled our hearts and ditched our dreams bankrupt

at the last supper we were deceived

by our very own Judas

Tinder Love

Technology won't help you stumble upon me
You won't unearth my tender heart
Hanging out on an app

No match on eHarmony
No singles dating hookup site

If you want an encounter
You'll have to meet f2f
In *real* time
Arising synchronous

So don't send me messages on Facebook
Or photos on Instagram of your enlarged penis
I've seen oodles of those noodles

I'm into skin on skin
A recurring caress
       nuzzle on my neck
           transfer your pheromones like cologne

I want to breathe you into my cells
Inhale you like Nadi Shodhan pranayama
up one side of me and down the other

A fusion of emotions   interconnected
      Burrowing

St. Peter's Abbey

Nov 11, 2011

On Barnyard Way, corrugated steel buildings rest on the edge
of the coulee like crescent moons casting light on this blessed place.

One lone horse, his white star like a third eye, gazes my way; half-cannons
covered in recent snow, he yearns for the stroke of human hands on his
withers.

Beside the blue barn discarded shelving and lockers
have fallen like dead soldiers.

Chickadees crisscross over my head, black capped and curious,
they swoop down,
disappointed in me. I should have brought peanuts
       some offering—
their tiny yellow breasts beating
       beaks open
       waiting,
on this walk toward death
down the white spruce promenade

Father Leo, Father Roman, Father James
       lie in their final resting place
       waiting
       to forgive me
       waiting
       for me
       to forgive myself

Get an opt out

Cinderella wake up
you better get a prenup

when your white knight lets you down
you will be
astonished

what the hell happened
to my fairy tale life

when your white wedding dress is hanging
in the closet
swallowed by moths
your lips will whisper   *he left me*

some other woman will be
the focus of his attention
your glass slipper will not be picked up
by the same prince
again

he will conveniently have no assets
deny he consummated your marriage
maybe even annul the children
move to another country

anything

to avoid responsibility

and
you will be left
with nothing
not a thing

At the Guggenheim in Venice 2015

After almost getting raped in Rome
I took the train to Venice and stayed at the Rialto
with fabric wallpaper
and gondoliers below singing garishly

A tourist doing touristy things.
From a congested vaporetto
(choosing now to wear a man's cap and overalls)
I entered the crowded (Palazzo Venier dei Leoni)
Peggy Guggenheim Collection on the Grand Canal

First, in the gardens
to honor the place where
she and her fourteen dogs are buried and

Then, in a white room
Replete with Jackson Pollock paintings

I had not expected to be alone.

He crouched beside me and handed me a can of paint.

'Throw it' he said.

Dizzy, I splattered and felt his hand over mine.

Afterwards, on a white leather bench

I lay down.

And wept.

To a Blind Woman

I would give you my eyes
take them to romantic places
so you can look into his
see them flicker with delight
tingle his silky skin
with each small glance

I would give you my eyes
to regard each falling leaf
hold the orange and yellow
spot the stillness in the trees
lie hand in hand on the beach

I would give you my eyes
for you to capture every second
every shade of daylight
catch your reflection in the mirror
the morning after love

I would give you my eyes
for you to leave me blind

Off on a Tangent

I galloped through mental pause
well not actually galloped
charged
frantic like a wild horse
inside the corral

At night you hardly noticed
the sheets wedged to my body
I'm a mermaid
legs trapped
scaly
wet

Or no, I'm like a stuffed sausage
the ones with the skin still on
the ones you peel back before
broiling on the barbeque
crisp
exploding from
internal combustion
heat

Amendment

I love how you never quite finish things

I love how you leave your clothes on the floor
right beside the laundry basket

how you leave your glasses
where I can see them

how you leave your coat on the chair
so you can leave quickly

how you tell me you love me
and kiss me on the cheek

These battles we engage in remain
like brown age spots on bony hands

like memories on tracing paper
we keep in a box

too frightened to open
in case we can't remember

or don't want to
transform

Mother's Prayer

Thank God
I don't have to worry about you at night
listening for you to come home and
creep in the back door
hear the beep of the microwave when you've
got the munchies

I don't have to worry about high school exams
fickle relationships fading
sad phone calls from college
the stress of not knowing what you will be when you grow up

I don't have to worry that you will overdo it
police phoning to tell me they found you smoking pot in the school field
helicopter hovering overhead when the party got out of hand

I don't have to worry about competitive sports
watching your heart break while you
sweat for some son of a bitch

I don't have to worry about you driving in bad weather
getting mugged at some bar downtown
or chased on the LRT by three idiots with a knife

I don't have to worry that I didn't love you enough

Now that you are grown up
I thank God I don't have to worry anymore

Sweat

A few women sit by the fire
Tánishi

First door
there's no going back now

rocks hiss
I lurch backwards
your voice calms me
Ni meyáten sage
breathe
meditate

let my spirit figure out where it is

Second door
prayer

White folks give thanks for their families
how blessed they feel to live in a place called Canada

First Persons give thanks for health balance peace
Pray for their fallen children
      speak of loss   abuse   pain

a spirit beckons
chant chant

let me know your language

Third door
the mind

twenty-one rocks glow
sweetgrass smolders
skirt stuck to skin
steam   smoke
salty nkochishpiten

it is good for us to feel pain for a short time
to remind us of others who live in pain every day

I wait for your song
you are a medicine man
mist rises from your body
otina la michin

Fourth door
gratitude

It's time to get spiritual again
unrestrained real belly laughter
with ma soeur beside me

song of strong women
song of young girls

heat sizzles
sears my bones

In the small cabin
you take my awkward hand
our food is blessed
we share bannock and stew
begin to cross boundaries

Thanks so much for coming

Pe'itotekekména

let me heal

let us ask for forgiveness

You are my Sunshine

Bent fingers wrapped by everlasting bands
tap your legs
tightly
body sways
shoulders swing
to the beautiful Tennessee Waltz

eyes glisten
eyebrows lift
in recognition of
the time you danced with your sweetheart

two broken watches on your wrist
trinkets that help you remember
this earth you are still on

from your murky mind
these words you sing clearly

a sudden reminiscence
of how much you have lost

Numbers and Hallways

Mom
you are at the Regency Manor in Central Butte
you have your own room
101
all the things in your drawers
and closets
are yours

Mrs. Dennis is in room
124
you can go down and see her
down the other hall

One lady who comes to visit and
lives here
is
Mrs. Williams
127

The lady who eats
at your table
on your left
is Mrs. Wankel
117

You can watch TV
in the lounges
at the end
of
each
hall

That you died on a Sunday

For Bruce

We used to go for dim sum on Sundays
and walk afterwards
by the river
        a simple ritual

We were both philosophical back then
probably read too much
        Northrop Frye
and thought too much
        about why Wallace Stevens was the best poet ever

        What didn't you know?

You being the bright holder of all truth—always a patient teacher

You emitted words like a human thesaurus—swore you were not a poet,
yet you spoke in poems

You told me to let my poems do what they must do, let them declare their
own intentions step aside and let them speak

Always a listener, you thought others had a more interesting tale to tell

That you died on a Sunday is appropriate
I see you munching on steamed dumplings in heaven

And I'm still here
remembering you   sitting on the railing at the U of S
watching the young dilettantes drift by
head in hand
        your black hair winking in the sunlight

The Abyssinian Baptist Church Harlem

I've never been a fan of Jesus

and then the white gloves held out their hands

and you spoke of fools you never thought you would meet

and I'm sure you were talking directly to me

how the work I've done should speak for me
how I'll go on and on and on longer than
I expected to be walking on this earth
how living eternal life is going the extra mile
so put my best foot forward
how I better damn well be doing something worthwhile
how I better let the light shine *like the shadow that the wind blows away*

and the Baptist choir sang

*My help
comes from the Lord,*[5]
All my blessings that I'm possessing

and the white gloves passed collection plates

women shouted *hallelujah praise the lord*

all minds were cleared of presumption and know-it-all-ness
it was a day of honoring and a day of commitment
of fairness and forgiveness
of knowing what to say and how to behave and what to do

next

and then the white gloves held out their hands
shook real hard

Winter Ceremonies II

I drive twenty years to see you

Do Not Resuscitate on the whiteboard
Obit written

Frail blue veins
Bulge
Trace your blood path

Half awake
You smile
Mutter   *'you look more beautiful than ever'*

You still know how to hurt me
………..

After they told me
About the frontal lobe damage
I asked them to give you more happy pills
I wanted you to stop counting
the number of times the heat came on through the night
………..

You had been asking for your pipe for weeks
I finally brought it, against others wishes.
He's dying I said *what does it matter now*
You joked, *Well, lookee here! It's Santa Claus!*

Aren't you going to light it?
You said *I'll just hold it awhile*

I spoke about my kids' sports
Small victories
Surprised how you understood about loss
………..

My roommate, you say in a snarky voice.
He never talks…
You ask me to rub heat lotion on your sores
I can tell they will never heal

I miss my dog you cry and cry
You give me a list of things you need
Most I cannot bring
I say I'll be back
Soon

Acknowledgments

The following poems have been previously published:

"Animal Instincts," *Spring*. Saskatchewan Writer's Guild. Vol. 8, 2013, p. 30.

"Blank Canvas," *Bitterzoet Magazine*. Vol 1, Dec./Jan. 2013, p.7. media.wix.com/ugd/fccea9_c96a212b55f74c05b48d27bd337717b7.pdf.

"Childcraft Encyclopedia," *New Voices in Fiction, Nonfiction, Plays & Poetry*. Silver Birch Press. May 16, 2015. silverbirchpress.wordpress.com/2015/05/16/childcraft-encyclopedia-by-merrill-elizabeth-gray-me-as-a-child-poetry-series/.

"Holy Cow," *Vast Horizons, New Words*. Blue Skies Poetry. Feb. 2011. blueskiespoetry.ca/2011/02/17/holy-cow/.

"Kalem," *Joy Interrupted: An Anthology on Motherhood and Loss*. Fat Daddy's Farm Press. Nov. 2012, p. 126.

"Leaving earth before you planned," *Joy Interrupted: An Anthology on Motherhood and Loss*. Fat Daddy's Farm Press. Nov. 2012, p. 122.

"Little Wing," *Paradigm Shift*. Temenos. Spring, 2015, p. 4.

"Pack Your Bags," *Vast Horizons, New Words*. Blue Skies Poetry. Feb. 2011. blueskiespoetry.ca/2011/02/14/pack-your-bags/.

"Playing Doctor," *Four Ties Lit Review*. Vol 2, Issue 1. July 2012. fourtieslitreview.files.wordpress.com/2012/08/four-ties-lit-review-v-2_-i-1.pdf.

"See you tomorrow Hayden Carruth," *Misfit Magazine*. Issue No. 3, Late Spring 2013. misfitmagazine.net/archive/No-3/index.html.

"The Prize Cat," *Fieldstone Review*. Issue 5, July 2012. merrillelizabethgray.com/_files/ugd/6a0d11_c655fa2b9c4442eb85fc3d414cec61c4.pdf.

"They Said," *Joy Interrupted: An Anthology on Motherhood and Loss*. Fat Daddy's Farm Press. Nov. 2012, p. 105.

"Tight Pants Rant." *S/tick*. s-tick.tumblr.com/post/92832971305/merrill-edlund.

"When I miss my kids," *Joy Interrupted: An Anthology on Motherhood and Loss*. Fat Daddy's Farm Press. Nov. 2012, p. 103.

"Winter Ceremonies II" (adapted from "Mourning Glory"). *Grain Magazine — the Journal of Eclectic Writing*. Vol. 41, No. 3, Spring, 2014.

Works Cited

---

[1] Mensch, Fred. *Aspects of Heroism and Evolution in Some Poems by E.J. Pratt.* University of Lethbridge. A thesis submitted in partial fulfillment of the requirements for the degree of Master of Arts. 1972. p. 23.

[2] Mensch. p. 12.

[3] The Prize Cat: Annotations Box 7, no. 60. *On his life and Poetry* 95. trentu.ca/faculty/pratt/poems/annotations/134annotations.html.

[4] MacDonald, R. D. "E.J. Pratt: Apostle of the Techno/Corporate Culture?" *Canadian Poetry* 37, 1995. p. 17-41. canadianpoetry.org/volumes/vol37/macdonald.

[5] Psalm 121:2.

Printed in the USA
CPSIA information can be obtained
at www.ICGtesting.com
LVHW051507020124
767910LV00004B/643